Table of Content

Disclaimer 2
Introduction 4
What is Financial literacy? 6
How to calculate your net-worth? 7
Steps to Manage Finance 9
Creating a budget 11
How to start saving 13
How to start investing 15
Types of investing 17
How to manager your debt 19
Setting financial goals 21
How to educate yourself financially 23
 How to protect your assets 26
Living below your means 29
The importance of tracking you expenses 32
How to be flexible financially 34
Steps to prepare for retirement 37
How to use your credit card wisely 39
How to improve your credit? 42
Terms to know 45
Conclusion 50

Disclaimer

The information provided in this book is for educational and informational purposes only. It is not intended to be a substitute for professional financial advice. The author and publisher of this book are not financial advisors, and the content provided should not be construed as financial advice.

While every effort has been made to ensure the accuracy and completeness of the information presented, the author and publisher make no representations or warranties of any kind, express or implied, about the completeness, accuracy, reliability, suitability, or availability with respect to the content contained herein.

Readers are encouraged to consult with a qualified financial advisor or other professional before making any financial decisions. The author and publisher disclaim any liability for any loss or risk, personal or otherwise, incurred as a consequence of the use and application, directly or indirectly, of any information presented in this book.

Financial markets and regulations can change rapidly, and readers are advised to verify any information before relying on it. The opinions expressed in this book are those of the author and do not necessarily reflect the views of any organizations or institutions mentioned.

By reading this book, you agree that the author and publisher shall not be held responsible for any consequences resulting from actions taken based on the information provided.

Introduction

Welcome to "Managing Financing: A Comprehensive Guide to Financial Mastery". In today's dynamic economic landscape, understanding how to effectively manage finances is paramount to achieving stability, growth, and ultimately, freedom. Whether you're an individual striving for personal financial security or a business owner navigating the complexities of fiscal management, this book is your road map to success.

In the pages that follow, we will embark on a journey through the fundamental principles of finance, delving into strategies and tactics that empower you to take control of your financial destiny. From budgeting and saving to investing and risk management, each chapter is crafted to equip you with the knowledge and tools necessary to make informed decisions and optimize your financial outcomes.

But why is financial management so crucial? Beyond the obvious benefits of wealth accumulation and prosperity, mastering your finances affords you something far more valuable: peace of mind. By cultivating a deep understanding of financial concepts and adopting prudent financial habits, you not only mitigate the stress and anxiety associated with money matters but also lay the foundation for a secure and fulfilling future.

However, it's essential to recognize that managing finances is not a one-size-fits-all endeavor. Each individual or organization has unique goals, challenges, and circumstances that must be taken into account. As such, while this book provides valuable insights and guidance, it's crucial to adapt and tailor the strategies presented to suit your specific needs and objectives.

As we embark on this journey together, I encourage you to approach each chapter with an open mind and a willingness to challenge conventional wisdom. By embracing a mindset of continuous learning and improvement, you'll position yourself for financial success and unlock the doors to a brighter future.

So let's dive in and begin our exploration of managing financing—a journey that promises to transform not only your finances but your life as well.

What is Financial literacy?

Financial literacy refers to the ability to understand and effectively manage various aspects of personal finances. It encompasses knowledge and skills related to budgeting, saving, investing, borrowing, and protecting against financial risks. A financially literate individual is equipped with the understanding and tools necessary to make informed decisions about money matters, both in the short term and the long term.

Financial literacy involves comprehension of basic financial concepts such as interest rates, inflation, compounding, and risk diversification. It also encompasses practical skills like creating and adhering to a budget, setting financial goals, managing debt responsibly, and planning for retirement or other long-term financial objectives.

In essence, financial literacy is about empowering individuals to take control of their financial futures by providing them with the knowledge, skills, and confidence to make sound financial decisions that align with their goals and values. It is an essential life skill in today's complex and ever-changing financial landscape, contributing to financial stability, security, and overall well-being.

How to calculate your net-worth?

Calculating your network involves adding up all your assets (like savings, investments, real estate, etc.) and then subtracting your liabilities (like debts, loans, mortgages, etc.). The result gives you a snapshot of your financial position.

To calculate your net worth, follow these steps:

◆ **List all your assets:** Include everything you own that has value, such as savings, investments, real estate, vehicles, and valuable items like jewelry or artwork.

◆ **Assign values to your assets:** Use current market values whenever possible. For items like vehicles or valuable items, you may need to estimate their worth based on market value or appraisal.

◆ **List all your liabilities:** This includes debts like mortgages, car loans, student loans, credit card balances, and any other outstanding loans.

◆ **Assign values to your liabilities:** Use the current outstanding balance for each debt.

- **Subtract your total liabilities from your total assets:** This calculation will give you your net worth.

Formula: Net Worth = Total Assets - Total Liabilities

Knowing your net worth provides a clear picture of your financial health and can help you make informed decisions about your finances.

Steps to Manage Finance

Managing finances effectively involves several key steps:

- **Budgeting:** Create a detailed budget outlining your income and expenses. Track your spending to ensure you're staying within your budget each month.

- **Saving:** Establish an emergency fund to cover unexpected expenses, and save for long-term goals like retirement or buying a home.

- **Investing:** Learn about different investment options and consider investing in stocks, bonds, mutual funds, or real estate to grow your wealth over time.

- **Debt Management:** Prioritize paying off high-interest debt, such as credit card debt, while making minimum payments on other debts.

- **Financial Goals:** Set specific, achievable financial goals, and regularly review your progress to stay motivated and on track.

- **Education:** Continuously educate yourself about personal finance topics to make informed decisions and adapt to changing financial circumstances.

- **Protect Your Assets:** Safeguard your financial well-being by having adequate insurance coverage, including health insurance, life insurance, disability insurance, and property insurance. Review your insurance policies regularly to ensure they meet your current needs.

- **Live Below Your Means:** Practice frugality and avoid unnecessary expenses to live below your means. Cultivate a mindset of conscious spending and prioritize spending on things that align with your values and long-term goals.

- **Stay Flexible:** Be prepared to adapt to changes in your financial situation, economic conditions, and life circumstances. Flexibility and resilience are essential qualities for maintaining financial stability over the long term.

By incorporating these practices into your financial routine and staying committed to your financial goals, you can maintain a healthy financial status and build a solid foundation for your future financial success.

Creating a budget

Creating a budget involves several steps:

◆ **Calculate Your Income:** Determine your total monthly income, including salaries, wages, bonuses, and any other sources of income.

◆ **List Your Expenses:** Make a list of all your monthly expenses, including fixed expenses (like rent/mortgage, utilities, loan payments) and variable expenses (like groceries, entertainment, dining out).

◆ **Differentiate Between Needs and Wants:** Differentiate between essential expenses (needs) and discretionary expenses (wants). Focus on covering your needs first.

◆ **Assign Amounts:** Assign specific amounts to each expense category based on your past spending habits and financial goals. Be realistic but also look for areas where you can cut back if necessary.

◆ **Track Your Spending:** Keep track of your spending throughout the month to ensure you're staying within your budget. This can be done manually with a spreadsheet or using budgeting apps.

◆ **Review and Adjust:** At the end of each month, review your budget and compare your actual spending to your budgeted amounts. Adjust your budget as needed to account for any discrepancies or changes in your financial situation.

◆ **Set Aside Savings:** Allocate a portion of your income towards savings and investments, including an emergency fund and long-term savings goals.

Remember, creating a budget is a dynamic process, and it may take some time to find a system that works best for you. Keep refining and adjusting your budget as your financial situation evolves.

How to start saving

Starting to save can seem daunting, but there are several effective strategies to begin:

◆ **Set Clear Goals:** Determine what you're saving for, whether it's an emergency fund, a vacation, a down payment on a house, or retirement. Having clear goals will motivate you to save.

◆ **Create a Budget:** Establish a budget to track your income and expenses. This will help you identify areas where you can cut back on spending and allocate more towards savings.

◆ **Automate Your Savings:** Set up automatic transfers from your checking account to your savings account each payday. This way, you're less likely to spend the money before saving it.

◆ **Start Small:** If you're new to saving, start with a small, manageable amount and gradually increase it over time as you become more comfortable with saving.

- **Cut Expenses:** Look for ways to reduce unnecessary expenses, such as dining out less frequently, canceling subscriptions you don't use, or finding more affordable alternatives for everyday purchases.

- **Track Your Progress:** Keep track of your savings progress regularly. Seeing your savings grow can be motivating and encourage you to continue saving.

- **Emergency Fund:** Prioritize building an emergency fund to cover unexpected expenses, like medical bills or car repairs. Aim to save enough to cover 3-6 months' worth of living expenses.

Consistency is key when it comes to saving. Even small contributions can add up over time, so don't get discouraged if you can't save a large amount right away. The important thing is to get started and make saving a habit.

How to start investing

- **Educate Yourself:** Take the time to learn about different investment options, basic financial concepts, and how the stock market works. There are many resources available online, including books, courses, and reputable financial websites.

- **Start with a Plan:** Define your investment goals, time horizon, and risk tolerance. Having a clear plan will help guide your investment decisions and keep you focused on your objectives.

- **Start Small:** Begin with a small amount of money that you can afford to invest. As you gain confidence and experience, you can gradually increase your investment contributions.

- **Diversify Your Portfolio:** Spread your investments across different asset classes, such as stocks, bonds, and real estate, to reduce risk. Diversification can help minimize the impact of market fluctuations on your overall portfolio.

- **Invest for the Long Term:** Avoid trying to time the market or chasing short-term gains. Instead, focus on building a diversified portfolio of quality investments and staying invested for the long term.

- **Stay Calm During Market Volatility:** Market fluctuations are normal, and it's essential to remain calm and avoid making impulsive decisions based on emotions. Stick to your investment plan and avoid reacting to short-term market movements.

- **Monitor and Review Your Investments:** Regularly review your investment portfolio to ensure it remains aligned with your goals and risk tolerance. Re-balance your portfolio if necessary to maintain diversification.

- **Consider Tax Implications:** Be mindful of the tax implications of your investments, especially regarding capital gains taxes and tax-deferred retirement accounts. Consult with a tax advisor if needed to optimize your tax strategy.

- **Stay Patient and Persistent:** Building wealth through investing takes time and patience. Stay disciplined, stay invested, and focus on the long-term growth of your investments.

Remember, investing involves risks, and there are no guarantees of returns. Be prepared to weather market fluctuations and stay committed to your long-term investment strategy. If you're unsure about where to start, consider consulting with a financial advisor for personalized guidance.

Types of investing

- **Stocks:** Investing in individual stocks allows you to own a portion of a company's shares. Stocks have the potential for high returns but also come with higher risk. Diversifying your stock portfolio can help spread risk.

- **Bonds:** Bonds are debt securities issued by governments or corporations. They typically offer lower returns compared to stocks but are generally less volatile. Bonds can provide a steady income stream through interest payments.

- **Mutual Funds:** Mutual funds pool money from multiple investors to invest in a diversified portfolio of stocks, bonds, or other securities. They are managed by professional fund managers and offer diversification with lower investment minimums.

- **Exchange-Traded Funds (ETFs):** Similar to mutual funds, ETFs also offer a diversified portfolio of stocks, bonds, or commodities. They trade on stock exchanges like individual stocks and often have lower fees than mutual funds.

- **Real Estate:** Investing in real estate can provide rental income and potential appreciation in property value. Options include buying rental properties, real estate investment trusts (REITs), or real estate crowdfunding platforms.

- ◆ **Retirement Accounts:** Take advantage of tax-advantaged retirement accounts like 401(k)s, IRAs, or Roth IRAs. These accounts offer tax benefits and can help you save for retirement.

- ◆ **Robo-Advisors:** Robo-advisors are automated investment platforms that use algorithms to create and manage investment portfolios based on your financial goals and risk tolerance. They often have lower fees compared to traditional financial advisors.

- ◆ **Peer-to-Peer Lending:** Peer-to-peer lending platforms allow you to lend money to individuals or small businesses in exchange for interest payments. It can provide diversification and potentially higher returns than traditional fixed-income investments.

Before investing, it's essential to do your research, understand the risks involved, and consider seeking advice from a financial advisor. Additionally, diversifying your investments across different asset classes can help spread risk and improve long-term returns.

How to manager your debt

Managing debt effectively involves several steps to regain control of your finances:

◆ **Assess Your Debt:** Start by gathering information about all your debts, including the total amount owed, interest rates, and minimum monthly payments. This will give you a clear picture of your financial situation.

◆ **Prioritize Your Debts:** Rank your debts based on interest rates, with higher interest debts being the priority. Focus on paying off high-interest debts first while making minimum payments on others to avoid accumulating more interest.

◆ **Create a Repayment Plan:** Develop a repayment plan that fits your budget and allows you to pay off debts systematically. Consider using the debt snowball method (paying off the smallest debts first) or the debt avalanche method (paying off the highest interest debts first).

◆ **Reduce Expenses:** Look for ways to cut back on expenses to free up more money for debt repayment. This may involve budgeting, reducing discretionary spending, or finding ways to increase your income through side hustles or freelance work.

◆ **Negotiate with Creditors:** Reach out to your creditors to negotiate lower interest rates, reduced monthly payments, or alternative repayment plans if you're struggling to make payments. Many creditors are willing to work with you to find a solution.

◆ **Consolidate Debt:** Consider consolidating multiple debts into a single loan with a lower interest rate, such as a personal loan or a balance transfer credit card. This can simplify your payments and potentially reduce your overall interest costs.

◆ **Build an Emergency Fund:** While focusing on debt repayment, it's essential to also set aside some money for emergencies. Having an emergency fund can prevent you from going further into debt when unexpected expenses arise.

◆ **Seek Professional Help if Needed:** If you're overwhelmed by debt and struggling to make progress on your own, consider seeking help from a reputable credit counseling agency or financial advisor. They can provide guidance and assistance in developing a debt management plan tailored to your needs.

Managing debt requires discipline, patience, and persistence. By taking proactive steps to address your debts, you can gradually work towards becoming debt-free and improving your financial well-being.

Setting financial goals

Setting financial goals is an essential step in achieving financial success. Here's how to do it effectively:

◆ **Identify Your Priorities:** Determine what matters most to you financially. This could include paying off debt, saving for retirement, buying a home, starting a business, or traveling the world.

◆ **Be Specific:** Set clear and specific financial goals. Instead of saying, "I want to save money," specify how much you want to save and by when. For example, "I want to save $10,000 for a down payment on a house within the next two years."

◆ **Make Them Measurable:** Your goals should be measurable so that you can track your progress. Break down larger goals into smaller, manageable milestones. For instance, if your goal is to save $10,000 in two years, aim to save approximately $417 each month.

◆ **Set Realistic Goals:** While it's essential to dream big, be realistic about what you can achieve given your current financial situation. Setting unrealistic goals can lead to frustration and disappointment.

Consider factors such as your income, expenses, and existing financial obligations when setting goals.

- **Establish a Timeframe:** Determine a timeline for achieving each goal. Whether it's short-term (less than one year), medium-term (one to five years), or long-term (more than five years), having a timeframe will help you stay focused and motivated.

- **Prioritize Your Goals:** If you have multiple financial goals, prioritize them based on their importance and urgency. Focus on tackling one goal at a time while making progress towards others.

- **Write Them Down:** Putting your goals in writing makes them more tangible and increases your commitment to achieving them. Display your goals somewhere visible, such as on a bulletin board or refrigerator, to serve as a constant reminder of what you're working towards.

- **Review and Adjust:** Regularly review your financial goals to assess your progress and make any necessary adjustments. Life circumstances and financial priorities may change over time, so it's essential to adapt your goals accordingly.

By setting clear, achievable financial goals, you can take control of your finances and work towards building the future you desire. Remember to celebrate your achievements along the way and stay motivated to pursue your financial dreams.

How to educate yourself financially

Educating yourself financially is crucial for making informed decisions and achieving financial stability. Here are some effective ways to do it:

- **Read Books:** There are countless books available on personal finance topics, covering everything from budgeting and saving to investing and retirement planning. Look for highly regarded titles by reputable authors to expand your knowledge.

- **Take Online Courses:** Many websites offer free or paid online courses on various financial topics. Platforms like Coursera, Udemy, and Khan Academy offer courses taught by experts in finance and economics.

- **Follow Financial Blogs and Websites:** Subscribe to financial blogs and websites that provide valuable information and insights on personal finance topics. Websites like Investopedia, The Motley Fool, and NerdWallet offer articles, guides, and tools to help you learn about finance.

- **Attend Workshops and Seminars:** Look for workshops, seminars, or webinars hosted by financial experts in your community or online.

These events often cover specific topics in-depth and provide opportunities for interaction and Q&A sessions.

◆ **Listen to Podcasts:** Podcasts are a convenient way to learn about personal finance while on the go. There are many podcasts dedicated to financial topics, offering advice, interviews, and discussions on various aspects of finance.

◆ **Join Online Forums:** Participate in online forums and communities focused on personal finance, where you can ask questions, share experiences, and learn from others. Reddit's personal finance subreddit and Bogleheads forum are popular options.

◆ **Consult Financial Advisors:** If you have specific questions or need personalized guidance, consider consulting with a financial advisor. A qualified advisor can help you develop a financial plan tailored to your goals and circumstances.

◆ **Stay Informed:** Keep up with financial news and developments by following reputable financial news outlets, such as CNBC, Bloomberg, or The Wall Street Journal. Understanding current events and market trends can help you make informed decisions about your finances.

◆ **Practice Financial Management:** Apply what you learn by practicing good financial habits in your daily life. Create a budget, start saving and investing, and monitor your progress regularly. Hands-on experience is often the best teacher.

By taking advantage of these resources and actively seeking out opportunities to learn about personal finance, you can empower yourself to make smart financial decisions and achieve your financial goals.

How to protect your assets

Protecting your assets is crucial for safeguarding your financial well-being. Here are some strategies to help protect your assets:

◆ **Insurance:** Obtain adequate insurance coverage to protect against unforeseen events. This may include health insurance, life insurance, disability insurance, homeowner's or renter's insurance, auto insurance, and liability insurance. Review your insurance policies regularly to ensure they provide sufficient coverage for your needs.

◆ **Estate Planning:** Create an estate plan to ensure your assets are distributed according to your wishes in the event of your death or incapacitation. This may involve drafting a will, establishing trusts, naming beneficiaries for retirement accounts and insurance policies, and assigning powers of attorney.

◆ **Asset Protection Trusts:** Consider setting up asset protection trusts to shield your assets from creditors and legal judgments. These trusts can provide a layer of protection against potential lawsuits and creditors' claims while allowing you to retain some control over your assets.

- ◆ **Business Entities:** If you own a business or investment properties, consider structuring them as separate legal entities, such as corporations or limited liability companies (LLCs). This can help protect your personal assets from business-related liabilities and lawsuits.

- ◆ **Homestead Exemption:** Take advantage of homestead exemption laws in your state, which protect a portion of your home's equity from creditors in the event of bankruptcy or other financial difficulties.

- ◆ **Retirement Accounts:** Funds held in qualified retirement accounts, such as 401(k)s, IRAs, and pension plans, are typically protected from creditors under federal and state laws. Maximize contributions to these accounts to shelter your assets from potential creditors.

- ◆ **Asset Protection Strategies:** Explore other asset protection strategies, such as gifting assets to family members, using annuities, purchasing umbrella insurance policies, or investing in exempt assets like retirement accounts and certain types of life insurance policies.

- ◆ **Legal Advice:** Consult with a qualified attorney who specializes in asset protection and estate planning to develop a comprehensive asset protection strategy tailored to your unique circumstances and financial goals.

◆ **Maintain Good Financial Practices:** Practice good financial habits, such as paying bills on time, avoiding excessive debt, and conducting regular financial checkups to monitor your assets and liabilities.

◆ **Stay Informed:** Stay informed about changes in laws and regulations related to asset protection and estate planning, and adjust your strategies accordingly to ensure ongoing protection of your assets.

By implementing these asset protection strategies and seeking professional guidance as needed, you can help safeguard your assets and protect your financial well-being for the long term.

Living below your means

Living below your means involves spending less than you earn, allowing you to save and invest for the future. Here are some practical ways to achieve this:

◆ **Create a Budget:** Start by tracking your income and expenses to understand where your money is going. Then, create a budget that prioritizes essential expenses like housing, utilities, groceries, and transportation while allocating a portion of your income towards savings and debt repayment.

◆ **Cut Discretionary Spending:** Identify non-essential expenses that you can reduce or eliminate. This might include dining out less frequently, canceling unused subscriptions or memberships, buying generic brands instead of name brands, and finding free or low-cost alternatives for entertainment and leisure activities.

◆ **Avoid Impulse Purchases:** Before making a purchase, especially for expensive items, take time to consider whether it's a need or a want. Avoid making impulse purchases by waiting 24 hours or longer before buying non-essential items. This gives you time to evaluate whether the purchase aligns with your financial goals.

- ◆ **Comparison Shop:** When shopping for goods and services, compare prices from different vendors to find the best deals. Look for discounts, coupons, and sales, and consider buying used or refurbished items instead of new ones to save money.

- ◆ **Limit Credit Card Use:** Use credit cards responsibly and avoid carrying balances from month to month, as interest charges can quickly add up. Pay off your credit card balances in full each month to avoid paying unnecessary interest fees.

- ◆ **Negotiate Bills:** Negotiate with service providers, such as cable companies, internet providers, and insurance companies, to lower your monthly bills. You may be able to get better rates by threatening to switch providers or by bundling services.

- ◆ **Downsize Housing:** Consider downsizing to a smaller, more affordable home or apartment if your current housing costs are too high. Moving to a less expensive area or finding a roommate can also help reduce housing expenses.

- ◆ **Reduce Transportation Costs:** Cut down on transportation expenses by using public transit, carpooling, biking, or walking whenever possible. Consider downsizing to a more fuel-efficient vehicle or eliminating a car altogether if you live in an area with good public transportation options.

- **Increase Income:** Look for opportunities to increase your income through side hustles, freelance work, overtime, or career advancement. Use any additional income to boost your savings and investments rather than increasing your spending.

- **Stay Focused on Goals:** Keep your long-term financial goals in mind and remind yourself of the benefits of living below your means, such as financial security, reduced stress, and the ability to achieve your goals faster. Stay disciplined and consistent in your spending habits to maintain a lifestyle that aligns with your priorities.

The importance of tracking you expenses

Tracking your expenses is crucial for several reasons:

◆ **Awareness:** Tracking expenses helps you become aware of where your money is going. It reveals spending patterns and habits, allowing you to identify areas where you may be overspending or where you can cut back.

◆ **Budgeting:** By understanding your spending habits, you can create a realistic budget that aligns with your financial goals. Tracking expenses helps you allocate funds appropriately, prioritize spending, and avoid living beyond your means.

◆ **Control:** Tracking expenses gives you greater control over your finances. It helps you make informed decisions about discretionary spending, avoid impulse purchases, and stay accountable to your financial plan.

◆ **Goal-setting:** When you know where your money is going, you can set specific financial goals and track your progress towards achieving them. Whether it's saving for a vacation, paying off debt, or building an emergency fund, tracking expenses provides valuable insights into your financial journey.

◆

- **Financial Awareness:** Regularly tracking expenses fosters financial awareness and mindfulness. It encourages responsible spending habits, encourages you to think critically about your purchases, and empowers you to make informed financial decisions.

Overall, tracking expenses is a fundamental practice for effective financial management. It provides clarity, control, and direction, ultimately helping you achieve greater financial stability and success

How to be flexible financially

Being flexible financially involves adapting to changes in your financial situation, goals, and external factors while maintaining stability and progress towards your objectives. Here are some strategies to help you become more flexible financially:

◆ **Build an Emergency Fund:** Establish an emergency fund to cover unexpected expenses or income disruptions. Aim to save 3-6 months' worth of living expenses in a readily accessible account to provide a financial cushion during emergencies.

◆ **Diversify Income Sources:** Explore multiple sources of income to diversify your earnings and reduce reliance on a single source. This could include side hustles, freelance work, rental income, dividends, interest, or passive income streams.

◆ **Create a Flexible Budget:** Develop a budget that allows for flexibility in spending and saving. Allocate funds to essential expenses, savings, and debt repayment while leaving room for discretionary spending and adjustments as needed.

- **Adapt to Changing Circumstances:** Be prepared to adjust your financial plan and priorities in response to changes in your life circumstances, such as job loss, career changes, marriage, divorce, or unexpected expenses. Stay flexible and open-minded about alternative solutions and opportunities.

- **Monitor and Review Regularly:** Regularly review your financial situation, goals, and progress towards achieving them. Monitor changes in income, expenses, investment performance, and market conditions, and make adjustments to your financial plan as necessary.

- **Maintain Liquid Assets:** Keep a portion of your assets in liquid investments, such as cash, savings accounts, or short-term investments, that can be easily accessed without penalties or delays. This provides flexibility to cover short-term needs or take advantage of investment opportunities.

- **Manage Debt Responsibly:** Be cautious when taking on debt and avoid overextending yourself financially. Prioritize paying off high-interest debt, but also consider the flexibility of low-interest debt for strategic purposes, such as investing in higher-return opportunities.

- **Stay Informed:** Stay informed about changes in tax laws, economic conditions, investment trends, and personal finance strategies. Continuously educate yourself about financial topics to make informed decisions and adapt to evolving circumstances.

- **Seek Professional Advice:** Consult with financial advisors, tax professionals, or other experts for personalized guidance and advice on managing your finances effectively. They can provide insights, strategies, and solutions tailored to your specific needs and goals.

- **Stay Resilient:** Cultivate a resilient mindset and remain adaptable in the face of financial challenges or setbacks. Focus on solutions rather than dwelling on problems, and be proactive in finding ways to overcome obstacles and achieve your financial objectives.

By implementing these strategies and cultivating flexibility in your financial approach, you can navigate changes and uncertainties with greater confidence and resilience, ultimately achieving greater financial stability and success.

Steps to prepare for retirement

- **Set Clear Retirement Goals:** Determine your retirement lifestyle goals, including where you want to live, how you want to spend your time, and any specific activities or hobbies you want to pursue.

- **Estimate Your Retirement Expenses:** Calculate your expected expenses in retirement, including housing, healthcare, transportation, and leisure activities. Don't forget to account for inflation and potential healthcare costs.

- **Assess Your Retirement Income Sources:** Identify all potential sources of retirement income, such as Social Security, pensions, retirement accounts (e.g., 401(k), IRA), and other investments.

- **Create a Retirement Savings Plan:** Based on your estimated expenses and income sources, develop a savings plan to reach your retirement goals. Consider using retirement calculators or consulting with a financial advisor to help you determine how much you need to save.

- **Maximize Retirement Savings Contributions:** Contribute as much as possible to retirement accounts such as 401(k)s, IRAs, and other tax-advantaged savings plans. Take advantage of employer matching contributions if available.

- **Diversify Your Investment Portfolio:** Invest your retirement savings in a diversified portfolio of assets to manage risk and maximize returns. Consider your risk tolerance, time horizon, and retirement goals when selecting investments.

- **Review and Adjust Your Retirement Plan Regularly:** Regularly review your retirement plan and make adjustments as needed based on changes in your financial situation, goals, or market conditions.

- **Consider Healthcare and Long-Term Care Costs:** Factor in potential healthcare and long-term care costs in your retirement plan. Consider purchasing long-term care insurance to help cover these expenses.

- **Pay Off Debt:** Aim to pay off high-interest debt before retirement to reduce financial burdens and free up more money for savings and retirement expenses.

- **Develop a Withdrawal Strategy:** Plan how you will withdraw money from your retirement accounts in retirement to minimize taxes and ensure your savings last throughout your retirement years.

- **Consider Part-Time Work:** If possible, consider working part-time in retirement to supplement your income and stay engaged.

How to use your credit card wisely

Using a credit card responsibly can be a valuable financial tool that offers convenience, rewards, and the opportunity to build a positive credit history. Here are some tips on how to properly use a credit card:

- **Understand Your Credit Card Terms:** Familiarize yourself with the terms and conditions of your credit card, including the interest rate, fees, grace period, and rewards program (if applicable).

- **Create a Budget:** Establish a budget that outlines your monthly income and expenses. Use your credit card for purchases within your budget and avoid overspending.

- **Pay Your Balance in Full:** Aim to pay your credit card balance in full each month to avoid paying interest. If you carry a balance, you'll incur interest charges that can quickly accumulate and lead to debt.

- **Pay On Time:** Make at least the minimum payment on your credit card bill by the due date each month to avoid late fees and negative impacts on your credit score. Setting up automatic payments can help ensure you never miss a payment.

- **Monitor Your Spending:** Keep track of your credit card transactions and monitor your spending regularly. This will help you stay within your budget and identify any unauthorized charges or errors.

- **Use Credit Wisely:** Only use your credit card for purchases you can afford to pay off. Avoid using it for impulse buys or unnecessary expenses.

- **Avoid Cash Advances:** Cash advances typically come with high fees and interest rates, so it's best to avoid using your credit card for cash withdrawals unless absolutely necessary.

- **Utilize Rewards:** If your credit card offers rewards or cashback, take advantage of them by using your card for everyday purchases. Just be sure to pay off your balance in full each month to avoid negating the benefits with interest charges.

- **Keep Your Credit Utilization Low:** Aim to keep your credit utilization ratio—the amount of credit you're using compared to your total available credit—below 30%. This can help maintain a healthy credit score.

- **Protect Your Information:** Safeguard your credit card information and be cautious when making online purchases or sharing your card details. Monitor your statements for any unauthorized charges and report them immediately.

- **Review Your Statements:** Regularly review your credit card statements for accuracy and report any discrepancies or fraudulent activity to your card issuer promptly.

By following these guidelines and using your credit card responsibly, you can enjoy the benefits of credit while avoiding the pitfalls of debt and financial stress.

How to improve your credit?

Improving your credit score can take time and discipline, but it's an important step towards achieving financial health and securing favorable terms on loans and credit cards. Here are some strategies to help you improve your credit:

- ◆ **Check Your Credit Report:** Start by obtaining a copy of your credit report from each of the major credit bureaus (Equifax, Experian, and TransUnion) and review them for accuracy. Look for any errors or discrepancies and dispute them if necessary.

- ◆ **Pay Your Bills on Time:** Your payment history is one of the most significant factors affecting your credit score. Make sure to pay all your bills, including credit card bills, loans, and utilities, on time every month.

- ◆ **Reduce Your Debt:** Aim to lower your overall debt levels, especially revolving debt like credit card balances. Focus on paying down high-interest debt first and consider consolidating debt or negotiating with creditors to lower interest rates or payment terms.

- ◆ **Keep Credit Card Balances Low:** Try to keep your credit card balances well below your credit limits. High credit utilization—the ratio of your credit card balances to your credit limits—can negatively impact your credit score. Aim for a utilization rate of 30% or lower.

- **Don't Close Unused Credit Accounts:** Closing old or unused credit accounts can actually harm your credit score by reducing your available credit and increasing your credit utilization ratio. Keep these accounts open, even if you're not actively using them.

- **Limit New Credit Applications:** Avoid applying for multiple new credit accounts within a short period, as this can indicate financial instability and lower your credit score. Instead, focus on managing your existing credit responsibly.

- **Diversify Your Credit Mix:** Having a mix of different types of credit accounts, such as credit cards, installment loans, and mortgages, can positively impact your credit score. However, only take on new credit accounts when necessary and manageable.

- **Become an Authorized User:** If someone you trust has a credit card with a long history of on-time payments and low balances, ask them to add you as an authorized user. Their positive credit history can potentially benefit your credit score.

- **Use Credit-Building Tools:** If you're struggling to qualify for traditional credit cards, consider alternative credit-building options such as secured credit cards or credit-builder loans. These products are designed to help establish or rebuild credit.

◆ **Be Patient and Persistent:** Improving your credit score won't happen overnight, but with consistent effort and responsible financial habits, you can gradually see progress. Monitor your credit score regularly and celebrate your achievements along the way.

By following these strategies and maintaining good financial habits, you can work towards improving your credit score and achieving your financial goals.

Terms to know

- **Interest Rate:** The percentage charged by a lender for borrowing money or earned on invested money.

- **Principal:** The original amount of money borrowed or invested, excluding interest.

- **Loan Term:** The period of time over which a loan must be repaid.

- **Collateral:** Assets pledged as security for a loan.

- **Credit Score:** A numerical representation of an individual's creditworthiness.

- **Credit Report:** A detailed record of an individual's credit history.

- **Debt-to-Income Ratio (DTI):** The ratio of monthly debt payments to monthly income.

- **Amortization:** The process of gradually paying off a loan over time through regular payments.

- **Annual Percentage Rate (APR):** The total cost of borrowing money expressed as an annual percentage.

- **Secured Loan:** A loan backed by collateral.

- **Unsecured Loan:** A loan not backed by collateral.

- **Down Payment:** A portion of the purchase price paid upfront.

- **Equity:** The difference between the market value of an asset and the amount owed on it.

- **Mortgage:** A loan used to purchase real estate.

- **Refinance:** Obtaining a new loan to replace an existing loan.

- **Installment Loan:** A loan repaid in fixed installments over time.

- **Revolving Credit:** A line of credit with a maximum limit that can be borrowed against repeatedly.

- **Grace Period:** A period during which no interest or fees are charged on a debt.

- **Default:** Failure to fulfill a financial obligation.

- **Bankruptcy:** Legal status of being unable to repay debts.

- **Foreclosure:** Legal process by which a lender repossesses property due to non-payment.

- **Credit Utilization Ratio:** The ratio of credit card balances to credit limits.

- **Co-signer:** A person who agrees to repay a loan if the borrower defaults.

- **Credit Limit:** The maximum amount a borrower can borrow on a credit card.

- **Line of Credit:** A flexible loan with a pre-approved credit limit.

- **Credit Card Balance:** The amount owed on a credit card account.

- **Minimum Payment:** The smallest amount a borrower must pay toward their debt each month.

- **Late Payment Fee:** A fee charged for making a payment after the due date.

- **Penalty APR:** A higher interest rate charged for late payments.

- **Credit Counseling:** Professional advice to help manage debt and improve credit.

- **Debt Consolidation:** Combining multiple debts into a single loan with a lower interest rate.

- **Debt Settlement:** Negotiating with creditors to pay less than the full amount owed.

- **Prepayment Penalty:** A fee charged for paying off a loan early.

- **Loan Origination Fee:** A fee charged by lenders for processing a new loan.

- **Closing Costs:** Fees associated with closing a mortgage or loan.

- **Variable Rate:** An interest rate that can change over time.

- **Fixed Rate:** An interest rate that remains constant for the duration of a loan.

- **Compound Interest:** Interest calculated on the initial principal and any accumulated interest.

- **Simple Interest:** Interest calculated only on the principal amount.

- **Balloon Payment:** A large final payment due at the end of a loan term.

- **APRC (Annual Percentage Rate of Charge):** The total cost of borrowing including fees and charges.

- **Payday Loan:** A short-term, high-interest loan typically due on the borrower's next payday.

- **Student Loan:** A loan designed to help students pay for education expenses.

- **Personal Loan:** A loan used for personal expenses.

- **Business Loan:** A loan used to finance business activities.

- **Cash Advance:** A short-term loan obtained through a credit card or payday lender.

- **Credit Freeze:** A security measure that restricts access to a person's credit report.

- **Garnishment:** Legal process by which a creditor collects a debt by obtaining a court order to seize property or wages.

- **Lien:** A legal claim against property as security for a debt.

- **Repossession:** Seizure of property by a lender due to non-payment.

Conclusion

In conclusion, "Managing Your Financing: A Road map to Financial Freedom" serves as a comprehensive guide to navigating the intricacies of personal finance and achieving long-term financial stability. Throughout this book, we've explored essential concepts, practical strategies, and actionable steps to help you take control of your finances and build a brighter financial future.

From budgeting and saving to investing and retirement planning, each chapter has equipped you with the knowledge and tools necessary to make informed decisions and optimize your financial outcomes. By understanding the fundamental principles of finance and adopting prudent financial habits, you're empowered to overcome financial challenges, seize opportunities, and achieve your financial goals.

But the journey to financial freedom doesn't end here. It requires ongoing commitment, discipline, and a willingness to adapt to changing circumstances. As you continue on your financial journey, remember the importance of regular assessment, adjustment, and continuous learning. Stay informed about financial trends, explore new opportunities, and remain vigilant in protecting your financial well-being.

Above all, remember that financial success is not just about accumulating wealth—it's about living a fulfilling and meaningful life. Use your financial resources to pursue your passions, support your loved ones, and make a positive impact in your community. By aligning your financial decisions with your values and priorities, you can achieve not only financial prosperity but also a sense of purpose and fulfillment.

As you close this book, I encourage you to reflect on the insights gained and take action to implement positive changes in your financial life. Whether you're just starting your journey or looking to refine your existing financial strategy, know that you have the knowledge and tools to create the future you desire. With determination, perseverance, and a commitment to lifelong learning, you can unlock the doors to financial freedom and live the life you've always dreamed of.

Thank you for joining me on this journey. Here's to your financial success and a brighter tomorrow.

www.ingramcontent.com/pod-product-compliance
Lightning Source LLC
Chambersburg PA
CBHW050245230526
45470CB00005B/2119